My First Book of
Transport

 Charlotte Guillain

Illustrated by Nigel Chilvers

A & C BLACK • LONDON

Published 2012 by A&C Black,
Bloomsbury Publishing Plc
50 Bedford Square, London, WC1B 3DP
www.acblack.com
www.bloomsbury.com

ISBN 978 1 4081 7819 5

Text © Charlotte Gullain 2012
Illustrations © Nigel Chilvers 2012
The moral rights of the author and illustrator have been asserted.

Printed in China by C&C Offset Printing Co.

This book is produced using paper that is made from wood grown
in managed, sustainable forests. It is natural, renewable and
recyclable. The logging and manufacturing processes conform
to the environmental regulations of the country of origin.

To see our full range of titles
visit www.acblack.com

1 3 5 7 9 10 8 6 4 2

Contents

Transport around us

How many different types of transport can you see?

From trains to planes and diggers to bulldozers – there are so many ways of moving people and things around! Are you ready to find out about some of the different sorts of transport that we use all over the world?

Read the clues on each 'What could it be?' page and then turn the page to find out the answer!

I can see something with a yellow and white face. Is that a big eye at the front? Is it some kind of giant insect?

What could it be?

It's a high-speed train!

High-speed trains travel much faster than ordinary trains. They move on special tracks that run in a straight line. Many high-speed trains run on electricity from lines above the tracks.

Look out for . . .

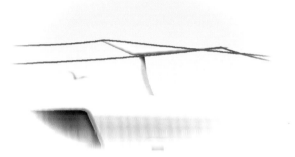

The **cables** connecting the train to electricity lines overhead.

The smooth, long, streamlined **driver's cab**.

The small **windows** that make the train more streamlined.

A large black shape splashes up through the surface of the sea. It's moving quickly through the water. Is it a shark or maybe a whale?

What could it be?

It's a submarine!

Submarines are ships that can travel under the sea!
They are shaped a bit like a fish so they can move easily
through the water. Submarines are used by the Navy and
also by scientists who study the ocean and its wildlife.

Look out for . . .

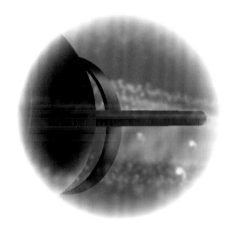

The **propeller** which pushes the submarine through the water.

The **rudders** which are used to steer the submarine.

The **periscope** which sailors under water can look through to see the surface.

I can see four long blades in a big cross shape. Is it a windmill? Or could it be a wind turbine for making electricity?

What could it be?

It's a helicopter!

The four blades on the top of the helicopter are called the main rotor. The main rotor spins round to make the helicopter fly. A helicopter can move backwards and sideways as well as forwards.

Look out for . . .

The **cockpit** where the pilot and co-pilot sit.

The **main rotor** which helps the helicopter to fly steadily.

The **winch** which is a machine that lowers a cable to rescue people.

The **tail rotor** which stops the body of helicopter from spinning round.

I can see a long shape moving down towards the ground. Is it a strange dinosaur's neck? The end of it scoops up soil and starts to dig.

What could it be?

It's a digger!

20

Diggers have to drive over rough ground on building sites. The large loader at the front scoops up and carries earth and gravel. It has powerful arms so it can lift up very heavy loads.

Look out for . . .

The **cab** where
the driver sits.

Big **tyres** which help
the digger move over
bumpy ground.

The **excavator arm**
at the back used for
digging.

The **stabilizer legs**
which hold the digger still.

I can see something moving up the mountainside. It's hanging in the air over the trees. Is it a strange tree house?

What could
it be?

It's a cable car!

24

People move up steep hills in cities and ski slopes in cable cars. Passengers stand or sit in a cabin, which hangs from overhead cables. An electric motor moves the cabin up and down the slope.

Look out for . . .

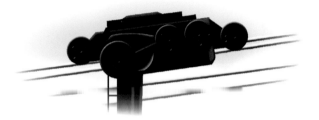

The **carriage** which moves the cabin along the cable.

The **cabin** where the passengers sit or stand to travel up the mountainside.

The **hanger** which attaches the cabin to the carriage above.

I can hear a sound like buzzing bees. It's getting louder. Is there a swarm of insects flying down this busy street?

What could it be?

It's a rickshaw!

Auto rickshaws are like little taxis with three wheels. The passengers sit on benches behind the driver. Rickshaws are small enough to move quickly in and out of busy traffic.

Look out for . . .

The **meter** which tells passengers how much they have to pay.

The **canopy** – passengers can lower the sides and the back depending on the weather.

The **spare tyre** in case there is a puncture!

Something is landing on the surface of a lake. Is it a huge bird? Water sprays out behind it as it comes to a stop.

What could it be?

It's a seaplane!

People use seaplanes to take off and land on water. The plane can float on the surface of the water. Seaplanes can fly to places that are hard to reach by car or boat.

Look out for . . .

The **propellers** which move the plane forwards through the air.

The **tail fin** and **rudder** which the pilot uses to steer the plane.

The **pontoons** or floats, which let the plane float on water.

Something is
moving quickly
through the snow!
It's zooming along
on the icy surface.
Could it be a bird
sliding on its tummy?

What could
it be?

It's a snowmobile!

Snowmobiles have special tracks that can move on snow and ice. They are a bit like motorbikes on skis. People use them to explore snowy places, or sometimes to race.

Look out for . . .

The ski-like **tracks** which run across the snow.

The **caterpillar tracks** which push the snowmobile forwards.

The bright **headlights** so people can see it coming!

I can see something long with bumps and ridges on it. It looks like a crocodile's back. It's moving quickly through the mud.

What could it be?

It's a bulldozer!

A bulldozer pushes dirt and rubble out of the way on a building site. It's a big, strong machine that can move on very rough ground. The cab where the driver sits looks a bit like a tractor.

Look out for . . .

The **blade** which can push almost anything out of the way!

The **ripper** which is like a claw that breaks up rock or earth into smaller pieces.

The **caterpillar tracks** which can move the bulldozer across bumpy surfaces.

Something is skimming across the sea. It looks like a metal stingray. It's moving quickly and silently through the waves.

What could it be?

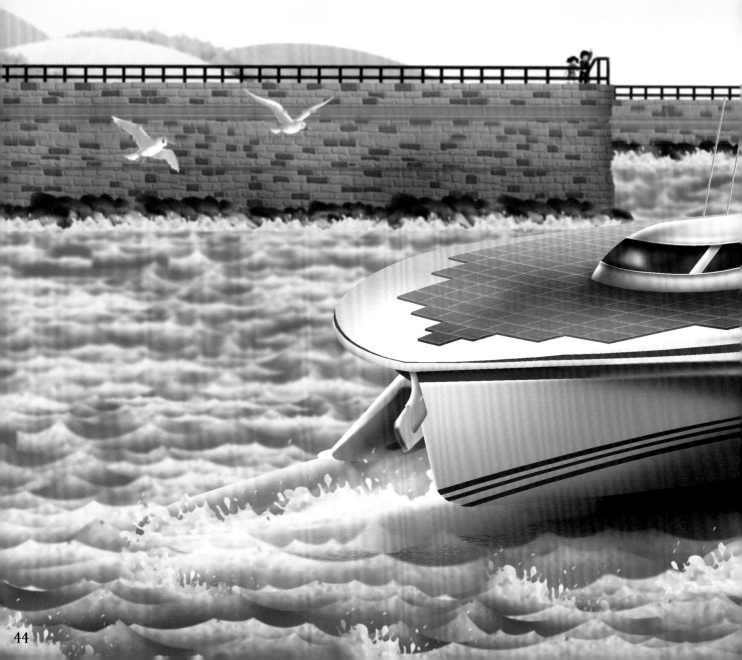

It's a catamaran!

A catamaran is a boat that floats on two hulls. It can move quickly and is stable in the water. This catamaran is powered by solar panels, using energy from the sun to move it forward.

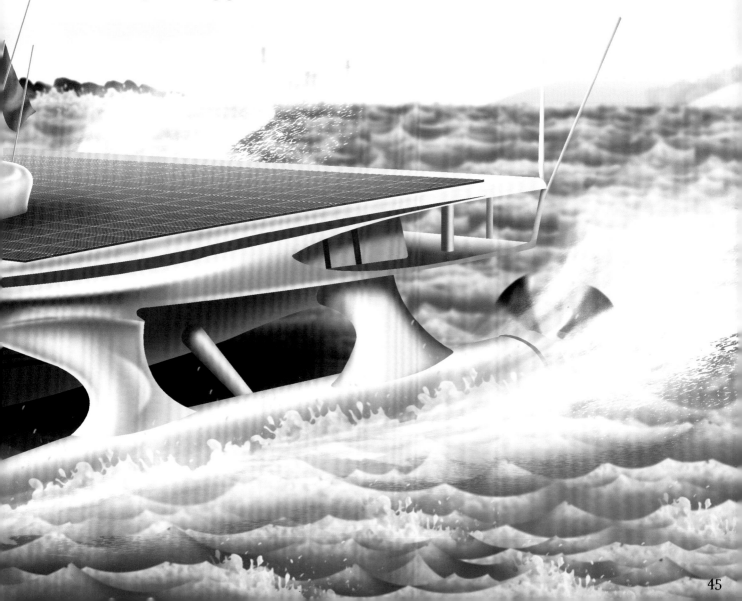

Look out for . . .

Propellers at the back of each hull.

Solar panels which use energy from the sun.

The **hulls** under the boat.

Transport words

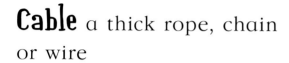

Cable a thick rope, chain or wire

Cockpit a place where the pilot sits in an aircraft

Float part of a vehicle that floats in water

Hull the body of a boat

Meter an equipment that calculates how much a passenger needs to pay

Periscope an instrument that people use to see what is above them

Propeller a machine with rotating blades that moves a vehicle

Rudder the flat part of a boat or plane that is used for steering

Solar panel a special panel that uses energy from the sun to make electricity

Streamlined shaped to move more quickly through air or water

Turbine a motor with blades

Winch a machine used to lift or pull things

Transport quiz

Now you have read this book, can you answer these questions about transport?

1. Why does a high-speed train have such small windows?

2. Why does a submarine need a periscope?

3. In what directions can a helicopter fly?

4. What is the excavator arm on a digger used for?

5. Where might you see a cable car?

6. How many wheels does a rickshaw have?

7. What is the pontoon for on a seaplane?

8. Why does a snowmobile have a caterpillar track?

9. What is a bulldozer used for?

10. What makes a catamaran stable in the water?